HUMAN RIGHTS AT RISK

REFUGEE AND IMMIGRANT RIGHTS

by Tammy Gagne

BrightPoint Press

San Diego, CA

© 2025 BrightPoint Press
an imprint of ReferencePoint Press, Inc.
Printed in the United States

For more information, contact:
BrightPoint Press
PO Box 27779
San Diego, CA 92198
www.BrightPointPress.com

ALL RIGHTS RESERVED.

No part of this work covered by the copyright hereon may be reproduced or used in any form or by any means—graphic, electronic, or mechanical, including photocopying, recording, taping, web distribution, or information storage retrieval systems—without the written permission of the publisher.

LIBRARY OF CONGRESS CATALOGING-IN-PUBLICATION DATA

Names: Gagne, Tammy, author.
Title: Refugee and immigrant rights / by Tammy Gagne.
Description: San Diego, CA: BrightPoint Press, 2025. | Series: Human rights at risk | Includes bibliographical references and index. | Audience: Grades 7-9
Identifiers: LCCN 2024004133 (print) | LCCN 2024004134 (eBook) | ISBN 9781678209308 (hardcover) | ISBN 9781678209315 (eBook)
Subjects: LCSH: Emigration and immigration law--United States--Juvenile literature. | Emigration and immigration law--Juvenile literature.
Classification: LCC KF4819.85.G345 2025 (print) | LCC KF4819.85 (eBook) | DDC 323.3/29120973--dc23/eng/20240214
LC record available at https://lccn.loc.gov/2024004133
LC eBook record available at https://lccn.loc.gov/2024004134

CONTENTS

AT A GLANCE	4
INTRODUCTION	6
FAMILIES TORN APART	
CHAPTER ONE	14
THE HISTORY OF IMMIGRANT RIGHTS	
CHAPTER TWO	26
IMMIGRANT RIGHTS IN THE UNITED STATES	
CHAPTER THREE	36
AN INTERNATIONAL ISSUE	
CHAPTER FOUR	46
THE FUTURE OF REFUGEE AND IMMIGRANT RIGHTS	
Glossary	58
Source Notes	59
For Further Research	60
Index	62
Image Credits	63
About the Author	64

AT A GLANCE

- Immigration has been central to US history. In the early 1800s, President Thomas Jefferson called for people from other countries to come to the new nation.

- Over the next 200 years, the United States created many laws that regulated immigration. Many of them favored white immigrants from Western Europe.

- The US Constitution gives noncitizen immigrants many of the same rights as US citizens.

- Many immigrants in the United States face discrimination. This can make it difficult for them to find jobs or housing.

- Immigrants also encounter problems in other parts of the world. Many of them experience human rights violations.

- Many people enter the United States illegally at the country's southern border with Mexico. Mexico also has issues with illegal immigration at its own southern border.

- Immigration has become a major political issue in the United States. Some people have criticized government leaders for mistreating immigrants to make political points.

- Some politicians are working to expand immigrant rights. They hope to improve how immigrants are treated in the United States through new legislation.

INTRODUCTION

FAMILIES TORN APART

In 2018, José Luis Martinez and his family came to the United States. They wanted a better life. The family traveled more than 2,000 miles (3,200 km) from Honduras. But when they arrived, US border officials took Martinez to a **detention center**. He asked where his children had been taken. But no one would tell him. Soon, Martinez was sent back to Honduras.

Refugees walk, cross rivers, and ride hidden in trucks to escape to safety in other countries.

Martinez's family was one of many families to be held at the border under a new policy. From 2017 to 2021, Donald Trump was president of the United States. He took a zero-tolerance stance on **undocumented immigrants**. These are people from other countries who enter the nation without permission. The policy became known as family separation.

Many undocumented families crossed the border into the United States. If police caught them, they arrested the families. Parents and other caregivers went to detention centers. Children went to separate shelters. The parents were not told where their kids were being held. Both parents and children worried. More than 5,000 children were taken from their families.

Refugee families who are stopped by US border patrol guards are taken to border patrol stations for a health and background check.

Some supported this policy. They thought it would stop families from coming to the United States illegally. But many people were against it. They said this was a violation of human rights. These are rights all human beings should have, no matter what race, religion, gender, or ethnicity they might be. Martinez reunited with his family in 2022. They were happy to be together again. But the pain they suffered from being separated lingered long after they were back together.

IMMIGRANT RIGHTS

Trump's policy started a debate about rights for those immigrants who have entered the country illegally. The separations were **traumatic** for families. And there was no process to unite families when their immigrant status was settled. Many adults were **deported**. But their children stayed in the United States. People protested the policy across the country. Trump stopped family separations in June 2018. Many of the families that were separated had

People around the nation protested the Trump administration's refugee policy.

War often forces a nation's citizens to flee to other countries for safety. Volunteers in host countries provide food, clothing, and shelter to refugees.

not been reunited. In 2021, President Joe Biden entered office. He was against separating immigrant families. He tried to reunite families. But more than two years later, about 1,000 kids were still separated from their parents.

Immigrants face many challenges in moving to a new country. Those who arrive without permission are at particular risk. Often they are trying to flee violence or poverty at home. Countries sometimes welcome these immigrants as refugees. Other times newcomers try to enter illegally and then seek protection. These immigrants often face abuse and other violations to their human rights. Countries around the world struggle with the best approach to these challenges.

CHAPTER ONE

THE HISTORY OF IMMIGRANT RIGHTS

The United States was founded in 1776 by immigrants. Most had come from Europe, specifically England, beginning in the 1600s. But not all the immigrants came to the continent freely. Some were sent as a punishment for crimes. People from Africa also came to North America. They did not come freely either. European slave traders brought them to the English colonies as **enslaved** people.

Immigrants from England arrived at Cape Cod, Massachusetts, on the *Mayflower* in November 1620.

The people who came to the colonies had different rights. White English citizens were treated best under the law. Criminals had few rights. But they could earn their freedom by working. Enslaved Black people had no rights. They could not earn their freedom. Andrew M. Baxter and Alex Nowrasteh are immigration experts. They say, "Thinking of [enslaved people] as immigrants stretches the meaning of that word to its breaking point."[1]

BUILDING A NEW NATION

The United States became a nation in 1776. More than a decade later, the US Constitution was passed. It included rules the country promised to follow. A Bill of Rights was added later. It promised people

Enslaved people who arrived in the colonies had no rights and cannot be considered immigrants.

certain rights. These included the freedom of religion and the right to free speech.

As more immigrants arrived, new laws were passed. The 1790 Naturalization Act limited immigrant rights. It stated that only free white people could become US citizens. But immigrants were needed to build the new nation. In 1802, Thomas Jefferson was president. He said, "The present desire of America is to produce

Immigrants arrived in the United States from countries such as Italy and Ireland in the early 1900s. Many entered the country at Ellis Island in New York.

rapid population, by as *great importations of foreigners* as possible."[2] The US Constitution gave immigrants the right to serve in government. But they could not be president or vice president.

Many people came to the United States between 1850 and 1920. The government passed immigration laws. Some limited the number of people who could come to the United States from certain countries. Other laws banned nonwhite people from immigrating. More people were allowed to come to the United States from northwestern Europe than from eastern Europe. For instance, more people from Norway were allowed to enter the United States than people from Poland.

Many immigrants were treated poorly. About 15,000 Chinese people arrived between 1863 and 1869. They came to

Birthright Citizenship

In 1868, the United States passed the Fourteenth Amendment to the US Constitution. It stated that all people born in the United States are US citizens. This right is called birthright citizenship. When someone who is not a US citizen gives birth in the United States, the baby is a citizen.

help build railroads. These workers were paid less than American railroad workers. Most Chinese workers were forced to sleep in tents. But American workers slept in train cars. By the 1870s, much of the work to build railroads across the country was complete. The government passed another law. This was the Chinese Exclusion Act. It banned Chinese workers from immigrating to the United States for the next 10 years.

EXPANDING IMMIGRATION ACCESS

The US government passed the Immigration and Nationality Act of 1965. The law allowed people with specific skills to come to the country. For example, doctors and scientists were needed. These people could

The US government has passed laws through the years to control immigration and protect immigrant rights.

immigrate if they already had job offers. Under the 1965 law, each nation had the same cap on the number of people who could immigrate. It favored immigrants who had family members already in the United States.

The Refugee Act of 1980 gave rights to those seeking **asylum** in the United States. Many refugees are forced to leave their nation during war. But the United States awarded refugee status only to certain people. These people were refugees, people who fled their countries to escape danger. Olga Byrne works for the International Rescue Committee. She explains, "A refugee is inherently a refugee even if a government hasn't yet made that determination."[3] People who are granted asylum in the United States cannot be forced to return to the place where they would suffer.

In 2012, Barack Obama was president. His administration created the Deferred Action for Childhood Arrivals (DACA) policy. This protects immigrants who were brought to the United States illegally as children. It allows them to remain in the country.

Those protected under DACA live in fear that they may be deported if the policy is not renewed.

Without DACA, many of these immigrants could be deported. DACA gave them a chance to become citizens. But DACA is not a federal law. The policy must be reviewed every two years. Politicians who support DACA are trying to turn it into federal law. Others are trying to prevent this from happening. In 2023, a Texas judge ruled that the most recent changes to DACA were unlawful. Current DACA immigrants were protected from being deported. But as of September 2023, there were cases in court that could end those protections.

Illegal immigration is a key issue for politicians and voters. President Trump wanted to stop people from illegally entering the country at the southern border. He ordered that the wall along the US border with Mexico be extended. Trump and many other Republicans thought the wall would help prevent illegal immigration. The United States spent $15 billion working on it. The new wall was 30 feet (9 m) tall in places. But many Democrats didn't think it would solve the problem. When President Joe Biden took office in 2021, 80 miles (129 km) of

Agents patrol the border between Mexico and the United States, but in some areas, thousands of people cross each day and there are not enough patrol agents to stop them.

new fencing had been added to the existing wall. He promised to stop the construction. But in October 2023, Congress ordered workers in Texas to keep building the wall. The border wall remains a highly debated issue.

CHAPTER TWO

IMMIGRANT RIGHTS IN THE UNITED STATES

The US government oversees immigration in the nation. It decides which people can legally enter the country. The government may deport people who enter illegally. Though they are not citizens, these people also have rights.

US Citizen and Immigration Services questions people who may have entered the country illegally. All immigrants have a right to a court hearing before they can

Immigrants are provided transportation to places to stay while they wait for their immigration hearings. Wait time for a hearing can be as long as 4 years.

be deported. Immigrants also have the right to an **attorney**. But the US government does not pay for this. Many immigrants receive hearings but do not have a lawyer.

Immigrants have other rights. One is to know the details of the crime they've been charged with. Another is to know when the hearing will take place. Immigrants who do not speak English have the right to an interpreter. Interpreters speak both English and the immigrant's language. They help immigrants communicate. The government must also prove that deportation is required by law before an immigrant is forced to leave the United States.

The US Constitution often uses the words *people* or *person* instead of *citizen*. This means that many rights are not limited

The Constitution of the United States guarantees certain rights, including freedom of religion and the right to free speech. These rights apply to anyone who lives in the country, not just citizens.

to citizens. People who enter the country illegally have the right to free speech. They have the right to freely practice religion. And they have the implied right to privacy.

Still, many people think immigrants are treated unfairly. One example is expedited removal. PBS *News Hour*'s Gretchen Frazee explains this process.

She writes, "Immigrants who have been in the country illegally for less than two years and are **apprehended** within 100 miles [161 km] of the border can be deported almost immediately without going through a court hearing."[4]

ASYLUM SEEKERS

Those seeking asylum have a right to a court hearing. They explain the dangers of staying in their home country. Then an immigration judge decides whether to grant asylum. A person given asylum becomes an asylee. Asylees are not citizens. But they are allowed to stay in the country. Asylees can get a job. They can travel in and out of the country. Asylees can also apply for their spouses and children to join them

Asylum seekers wait in line for food, clothing, and other basic needs when they first arrive in the United States.

in the United States. However, asylum is no guarantee. In 2021, more than 17,500 refugees asked for asylum in the United States. About 37 percent of them were granted it.

Immigrants who want to come to the United States can apply for a visa. This is a document that gives them permission to enter the United States. They can stay for up to 6 months. But asylum seekers can't be granted asylum before coming to the United States. Olga Byrne states, "There's no way to ask for a visa or any type of authorization in advance. . . . You just have to show up."[5]

COMMON PROBLEMS IMMIGRANTS FACE

Immigrants often face discrimination. This is the poor treatment of a person for an unfair reason. It makes it hard for many immigrants to find jobs. Some of them have to work very long hours. They also work in unsafe conditions. Sometimes they aren't even paid for all the work they do. Discrimination is against the law. But many immigrants do not know their rights. The US Department of Justice created the National

Immigrants may face hostile discrimination no matter where they relocate.

Origin Working Group. It helps immigrants learn more about their rights.

Sometimes state laws limit immigrant rights. For example, federal law states that

Refugees have a right to health care when they are sick. Sometimes, however, they are refused treatment.

public hospitals must treat all patients.

This includes immigrants. But a 2023

law in Florida made it more difficult for

undocumented immigrants to receive care. The law requires hospitals to ask patients if they are US citizens. More than half of undocumented immigrants are insured through a family member's policy. They can get care. Those without insurance worry that answering the question could get them deported. So they may not seek care.

Census Data and Immigrants

Every 10 years, the US Census Bureau collects data about who lives in the United States. People answer questions on a survey. However, many undocumented immigrants fear their responses could get them deported. Since 2020, the survey can't ask about immigration status. The information can't be shared with immigration agencies. These policies help ensure accurate census data.

CHAPTER THREE

AN INTERNATIONAL ISSUE

Immigration challenges are not limited to the United States. A lot of immigrants come to Mexico from Central or South America. Some continue north to the United States. Others want to stay in Mexico. In 2021, Mexico captured more than 300,000 people who entered the country illegally. About one-third of them asked Mexico for asylum. The country granted about 38,000 of these requests.

Immigrants and refugees from all over the world try to cross the border into the United States from Mexico. Many come from Central and South America.

One man made the trip to Mexico's southern border from Honduras. His home country has problems with gang violence. So do the nearby countries of El Salvador and Guatemala. The refugee feared for his life. He shares, "I never thought I would have to leave my country. Now, I know if I went back, I wouldn't last very long alive. If you don't obey the gangs there . . . they kill you."[6]

Refugees in Mexico must wait for an answer about asylum. While there, they may face discrimination. They often have trouble finding a job. Finding a place to live is hard, too. Some immigrants to Mexico come from Haiti. In 2010 Haiti had an earthquake. Since then, the country has faced severe

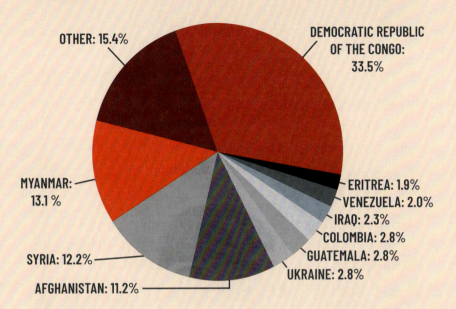

Source: Nicole Ward and Jeanne Batalova, "Refugees and Asylees in the United States," Migration Policy Institute, June 15, 2023. www.migrationpolicy.org.

Between October 2022 and May 2023, the most refugees arriving in the United States from one nation came from the Democratic Republic of the Congo.

poverty, hunger, and violence. But Mexico can't afford to support these refugees.

AFRICAN COAST

Africa's Mediterranean coast is a dangerous place for refugees. Many of those traveling from Africa to Europe along this route are attacked or killed. The Libyan Coast Guard often stops these refugees. It takes them to Libya instead. This nation is on Africa's

Authorities from Italy and other nations along the Mediterranean coast often rescue immigrants who are in danger of capture by the Libyan Coast Guard.

northern coast. Many of these people become victims of **human trafficking**.

People captured in other African nations also face human rights violations. Fatemah Ibrahim and others tried to make it to the Mediterranean coast from Nigeria. They were captured in Tunisia. She explained that the police hit them, took their phones and money, and arrested them. Activists in Tunisia have spoken out about its treatment of refugees. But the government has not changed its policies.

The trip to Europe is dangerous even for those refugees who avoid being captured. Refugees use small boats that flip easily in rough seas. Storms may tip larger boats, too. In February 2023, a boat filled with

Overloaded boats and rough seas mean refugees are often risking their lives to reach safety in a new land.

200 refugees sank on the way to southern Italy. At least ninety-four people died.

Between 2018 and 2023, more than 8,000 people died or went missing while crossing the Mediterranean Sea from Africa. About 1,500 of them were children. Catherine Russell is the executive director for the UN International Children's Emergency Fund. She states, "This is a clear sign that more must be done to create safe and legal pathways for children to access asylum, while strengthening efforts to rescue lives at sea."[7]

IMMIGRATION LAWS IN JAPAN

Japan has some of the strictest immigration policies in the world. In 2022, it allowed just 5 percent of refugees who applied for asylum to stay. In 2021, Japan passed a law against applying for asylum there more than once. People who apply three times or more will be deported. Amnesty International promotes human rights around the world. It believes this law violates refugees' rights.

Many immigrants to Japan go through the immigration process each year. Most come from other Asian countries such as China, Korea, and Vietnam.

Immigrants continue to enter Japan illegally. Some are kept in prisonlike facilities. People have told Amnesty International they suffered physical abuse. They did not have enough food. They were also denied medical care.

In 2021, asylum seeker Ratnayake Liyanage Wishma Sandamali died while being held in Japan. When she became sick, she asked to see a doctor. But the government said no. Then she asked to be released to get care. The government accused her of faking her illness. Many people in Japan were outraged over her death. The nation's Constitutional Democratic Party has tried to change the country's immigration policies. But so far, laws have only gotten stricter.

International Concern

The UN Human Rights Council works to stop human rights violations. In April 2023, the council told Japan that laws it was about to pass did not meet human rights standards. It urged the government to reconsider them. But Japan passed the laws that June.

CHAPTER FOUR

THE FUTURE OF REFUGEE AND IMMIGRANT RIGHTS

US politicians continue to debate immigration laws. Democrats and Republicans agree that illegal immigration is a problem. But they disagree about the best way to resolve the issue. In 2022, Texas governor Greg Abbott took action.

Abbott is a Republican. He said small border towns in Texas were being overrun with illegal immigrants from Mexico. He blamed President Biden and other

Under the direction of Texas governor Greg Abbott, immigrants boarded buses in Texas to cities such as New York, Chicago, or Denver.

Democrats for not fixing the problem. To bring attention to his cause, Abbott sent more than 11,000 undocumented immigrants out of his state on buses. They traveled to northern cities such as Chicago, Illinois; New York City; Philadelphia, Pennsylvania; and Washington, DC. Many elected leaders in these cities are Democrats. Abbott wanted these cities to experience the crisis he felt Democrats were causing in his state.

    Abbott said the immigrants had agreed to be moved to these cities. However, many saw this act as cruel and exploitative. Philadelphia mayor Jim Kenney accused Abbott of using immigrant families to play political games. Nonetheless, Kenney stated, "Philadelphia will greet our newly

Many US citizens are outraged by the treatment of the immigrants and refugees who come to the country. Calls for reform are common.

arrived neighbors with dignity and respect."[8] Many people condemned Abbott's actions.

SEPARATING IMMIGRATION FROM IMMIGRANT RIGHTS

Many people have strong feelings about immigration. Some see the United States as a nation of immigrants. To them, welcoming people from other countries is part of what the country is all about. Other people feel strongly that illegal immigration has gotten out of control. They think immigration strains US resources. But immigrant rights is a separate issue. Supporters of immigrant rights believe all people should be treated fairly and humanely. This includes immigrants, no matter what their status may be.

The American Civil Liberties Union (ACLU) protects the rights of all people in the nation. The ACLU's Immigrants' Rights Project was created in 1985. Attorneys challenge laws and practices that violate

American citizens have different views of immigration, but many believe that immigrants should have basic rights.

immigrant rights. The ACLU's website explains that the Constitution doesn't grant people from other countries permission to enter the United States. But it does protect them from discrimination once they are here.

EXPANDING IMMIGRANT RIGHTS

Many immigrants enter the country legally each year. Yet even they do not have all the same rights as US citizens. For example, only US citizens are allowed to vote in federal elections. Rules about local elections may vary by location. Washington, DC, allows permanent residents who are not yet citizens to vote in the city's elections.

Brianne Nadeau is a DC council member. She helped pass the law that allowed

The right to vote does not apply to people who are not US citizens. But some cities have passed laws to allow refugees and immigrants to vote.

permanent residents to vote in the city. She explains that these legal immigrants pay taxes and attend local schools. They are also active in the community. She says, "[W]ithout this legislation, they don't have a voice in our elections, which is essentially one of the most fundamental things in our country."[9]

Yet many US citizens do not think noncitizens should have this right. Several cities have passed laws allowing immigrants to vote. But some states passed laws to prevent their cities from doing the same. In Alabama, Colorado, Florida, Ohio, and Louisiana, immigrants cannot vote in state or city elections. In these states, immigrants must become **naturalized** citizens of the United States in order to vote. Then, they can vote in federal elections as well.

In May 2023, California congresswoman Linda T. Sánchez introduced the US Citizenship Act. This bill aimed to solve many immigration challenges. It focused on keeping immigrant families together. It also provided a way for undocumented immigrants to become citizens. But the bill

Before immigrants take the oath of allegiance to become naturalized citizens, they must pass English language and US history tests.

Those on both sides of the immigration issue have made their voices heard through protests or voting.

did not pass. Democrats and Republicans often disagree about immigration policies.

Immigrant rights in this country will likely be debated for a long time. People on both sides of the issue are determined in their cause. They want to make changes they think are needed. What becomes law will depend on which politicians are elected in the future.

No Longer a Crime

Some people want to make it legal for immigrants to enter the country to seek asylum or citizenship. They think this would stop immigration rights violations. In 1986, the US government passed the Immigration Reform and Control Act. It allowed those who had lived and worked in the country since 1982 to apply for citizenship. This solved the problem. But it wasn't a permanent solution.

GLOSSARY

apprehended
captured by law enforcement

asylum
official protection granted to a refugee

attorney
a person who practices law

deported
sent back to one's original country by another nation

detention center
a place where immigrants stay while waiting for hearings or deportation

enslaved
held against one's will and forced to work without pay

human trafficking
to force or trick someone to work for free or perform a sex act

naturalized
having gone through the official process to become a US citizen

traumatic
emotionally disturbing

undocumented immigrants
people who have entered a foreign country without permission

SOURCE NOTES

CHAPTER ONE: THE HISTORY OF IMMIGRANT RIGHTS

1. Quoted in Andrew M. Baxter and Alex Nowrasteh, "A Brief History of US Immigration Policy from the Colonial Period to the Present Day," *CATO Institute*, August 3, 2021. www.cato.org.

2. Quoted in "The Examination Number VII," *National Archives*, January 7, 1802. www.founders.archives.gov.

3. Quoted in "Is it Legal to Cross the US Border to Seek Asylum?," *International Rescue Committee*, October 6, 2023. www.rescue.org.

CHAPTER TWO: IMMIGRANT RIGHTS IN THE UNITED STATES

4. Gretchen Frazee, "What Constitutional Rights do Undocumented Immigrants Have?" *PBS News Hour*, June 25, 2018. www.pbs.org.

5. Quoted in "Is it Legal to Cross the US Border to Seek Asylum?," *International Rescue Committee*, October 6, 2023. www.rescue.org.

CHAPTER THREE: AN INTERNATIONAL ISSUE

6. Quoted in "Mexico: Asylum Seekers Face Abuses at Southern Border," *Human Rights Watch*, June 6, 2022. www.hrw.org.

7. Quoted in "Eleven Children Die Every Week Attempting to Cross the Central Mediterranean Sea Migration Route," *UNICEF*, July 13, 2023. www.unicef.org.

CHAPTER FOUR: THE FUTURE OF REFUGEE AND IMMIGRANT RIGHTS

8. Quoted in Brian Bushnard, "'Purposefully Cruel': Philadelphia Mayor Slams Texas Gov. Abbott as First Bus of Migrants Arrive," *Forbes*, November 16, 2022. www.forbes.com.

9. Quoted in Zachary Roth, "Noncitizens Allowed to Vote in Some Local Elections, Spurring Backlash from GOP," *Georgia Recorder*, March 14, 2023. www.geogiarecorder.com.

FOR FURTHER RESEARCH

BOOKS

Maliha Abidi, *Journey to America: Celebrating Inspiring Immigrants Who Became Brilliant Scientists, Game-Changing Activists & Amazing Entertainers*. Seattle, WA: Becker & Mayer Kids, 2022.

Tea Rozman Clark and Julie Vang, eds. *Immigrant Stories from Upstate New York High Schools*. Minneapolis, MN: Green Card Youth Voices, 2021.

Gail Radley, *Human Trafficking and Modern Slavery*. San Diego, CA: BrightPoint Press, 2025.

INTERNET SOURCES

"Asylum in the United States," *American Immigration Council*, August 16, 2022. www.americanimmigrationcouncil.org.

Claire Klobucista, Amelia Cheatham, and Diana Roy, "The US Immigration Debate," *Council on Foreign Relations*, June 6, 2023. www.cfr.org.

Trinh Q. Truong, "Why Immigration Relief Matters," *Center for American Progress*, February 1, 2022. www.americanprogress.org.

WEBSITES

ACLU Immigrants' Rights
www.aclu.org/issues/immigrants-rights

The American Civil Liberties Union defends and preserves individual rights and liberties guaranteed under the US Constitution and laws of the United States.

Amnesty International
www.amnestyusa.org

Amnesty International works for justice, equality, and the protection of human rights worldwide.

United Nations Human Rights Office of the High Commissioner
www.ohchr.org

This body of the United Nations works to resolve human rights violations around the world.

INDEX

1790 Naturalization Act, 17

Abbott, Greg, 46–50
American Civil Liberties Union (ACLU), 51–52
asylum, 21, 22, 30–32, 36, 38, 43, 44, 57

Baxter, Andrew M., 16
Biden, Joe, 13, 24–25, 46
Bill of Rights, 16–17
birthright citizenship, 19
border wall, 24–25
Byrne, Olga, 22, 32

census data, 35

Deferred Action for Childhood Arrivals (DACA), 22–24
deportation, 10, 23–24, 26, 28, 30, 35, 43
detention centers, 6, 8
discrimination, 19–20, 32, 38, 52

enslaved people, 14, 16

family separation policy, 8–10
Frazee, Gretchen, 29–30

health care, 33–35
human trafficking, 41

Ibrahim, Fatemah, 41
immigrant rights, 10–13, 17, 26–35, 50–57
Immigration and Nationality Act, 20–21

Japanese policies, 43–45
Jefferson, Thomas, 17–18

Kenney, Jim, 48–50

Martinez, José Luis, 6, 10

Nadeau, Brianne, 52–53
Nowrasteh, Alex, 16

origin of US refugees, 39

Refugee Act of 1980, 21–22
Russell, Catherine, 42–43

Sánchez, Linda T., 54–56
Sandamali, Ratnayake Liyanage Wishma, 44–45

Trump, Donald, 8, 10, 24

US Citizen and Immigration Services, 26
US Constitution, 16–17, 18, 19, 28, 52

IMAGE CREDITS

Cover: © Jim Newberry/Alamy
5: © Ajdin Kamber/Shutterstock Images
7: © Vic Hinterlang/Shutterstock Images
9: © Vic Hinterlang/Shutterstock Images
11: © Jana Shea/Shutterstock Images
12: © Maksym Szyda/Shutterstock Images
15: © Joseph Sohm/Shutterstock Images
17: © Morphart Creation/Shutterstock Images
18: © Library of Congress
21: © Tupungato/Shutterstock Images
23: © Sheila Fitzgerald/Shutterstock Images
25: © Poli Pix Co. LLC/Shutterstock Images
27: © Vic Hinterlang/Shutterstock Images
29: © Janece Flippo/Shutterstock Images
31: © Lev Radin/Shutterstock Images
33: © Ajdin Kamber/Shutterstock Images
34: © Pressmaster/Shutterstock Images
37: © David Peinado Romero/Shutterstock Images
39: © Red Line Editorial
40: © Alessio Tricani/Shutterstock Images
42: © Nicolas Economou/Shutterstock Images
44: © SubstanceTproductions/Shutterstock Images
47: © Marcel Nothdurft/Shutterstock Images
49: © arak7/Shutterstock Images
51: © Peter Sherman Crosby/Shutterstock Images
53: © Sharkshock/Shutterstock Images
55: © Lev Radin/Shutterstock Images
56: © Jana Shea/Shutterstock Images

ABOUT THE AUTHOR

Tammy Gagne is a freelance writer and editor who specializes in educational nonfiction for young people. She has written hundreds of books on a wide range of topics. Some of her favorite projects have been about human rights and racial injustices. Gagne resides in northern New England with her husband, son, and dogs.